The Power of Communion

The Power of Communion
Copyright © 2017 Derek Prince Ministries – International.
This edition published by Derek Prince Ministries – UK 2017

ISBN 978-1-78263-422-5

Kindle 978-1-78263-446-1

ePub 978-1-78263-445-4

Product code: B126

This book was compiled from the extensive archives of
Derek Prince's unpublished materials, and edited by
the Derek Prince Ministries editorial team.

Derek Prince Ministries
www.derekprince.com

Contents

Foreword

What answer would you give if someone were to ask you, "When did the first Communion take place?" Chances are good that your response would be something like this: "The Last Supper, of course. Everyone knows that!"

Most Christians would agree with you. However, you might be amazed at the answer Derek Prince provides in this book, *The Power of Communion*.

What you are about to learn in the opening pages of this book may surprise you. As Derek skilfully points out through the Scriptures, the Last Supper was not necessarily the first celebration of the Eucharist. The first exchange of bread and wine – the Communion elements – took place at an historical event thousands of years earlier.

It comes in a description of a battle in Genesis in which Abram, father of Israel, has achieved a victory. At that moment, Abram encounters a mysterious figure who comes out to meet him in the King's Valley on the hillsides east of Jerusalem. The enigmatic leader? Melchizedek, King of Salem. But Who is he really?

Derek's unusual beginning to his teaching about Communion will captivate your imagination, as will the entire study of the theme in this book. From his starting point in Genesis to the poignant scene with Jesus and His disciples in the Upper Room, Derek will lead us on a biblical journey into a deeper, richer understanding of this precious sacrament of Communion that we observe in honour of Jesus, just as He commanded.

Along the way, we will delve deeply into the mysteries of this solemn sacrament. Why are we asked to "eat" Jesus' flesh and "drink" His blood? Why was Jesus called a Priest forever after the order of Melchizedek? What changes take place in us when we take Communion?

These and many other questions are answered in the pages to follow. And one last comment: when you are coming to the end of the book, please don't stop. Keep reading! In some ways, Derek has saved the best for last. In the final chapters, Derek opens his life to us in a rare, touching and personal way. Through what he shares from some of the most difficult and yet gratifying moments of his life, you will discover what Communion meant to Derek Prince.

With tremendous biblical scholarship and deeply personal accounts, Derek Prince presents this theme in a way that will profoundly impact your relationship with Jesus Christ each time you meet Him at The Table of the Lord. That lasting impact of His profound love for you is our heartfelt wish and prayer for you as you read this amazing book – *The Power of Communion*.

The International Editorial Team
of Derek Prince Ministries

CHAPTER ONE

A Surprising Beginning

Some of the most beautiful, heart-rending words ever spoken by Jesus were these: "Do this in remembrance of Me." These are the words He spoke the night before His crucifixion as He was breaking bread with His disciples in the Upper Room.

During these last days of His life on earth, Jesus was very intentional. He was instituting for us the most highly treasured sacrament of our Christian faith. That is why I have chosen "The Power of Communion" as the topic of this book. It is vital for us as Christians to know some simple, basic truths from the Bible about this powerful sacrament: Communion, the Table of the Lord.

There are various names used amongst Christians for this sacred ceremony. Some of these are the Eucharist, the Lord's Supper, Communion, or the Table of the Lord. I believe all of these are beautiful names, and I wouldn't want to give up any of them. No matter which one I may happen to use, I want you to understand that if in your tradition you use a different name, we are still speaking about the same important sacrament.

An Intriguing Encounter

One might assume that any book on "The Power of Communion" would begin with Jesus and His disciples at the Last Supper, where Jesus instituted the covenant meal of bread and wine. However, I am going to surprise you.

I would like to begin our exploration of the subject of Communion by examining a passage from Genesis 14:17–24. These verses describe an intriguing encounter between Abram (whose name had not yet been changed to Abraham) and one of the most exciting and mysterious characters of the Old Testament, Melchizedek.

Before we look at these verses, let me point out that the name Melchizedek means "King of Righteousness." We are also told that he was King of Salem, which is the original name of Jerusalem (the first part of the name was added later). The word *Salem* is directly associated with the word *shalom*, which you may already know is the Hebrew word for *peace*. So by his name, this man was the King of Righteousness. By his location, he was the King of Peace.

Although there is a good deal said about Melchizedek in the epistle to the Hebrews, he still remains, at the end of it all, a somewhat enigmatic figure. Many believe that this appearance in Genesis 14 was a Christophany – that is, a pre-incarnation manifestation of Jesus. Others believe differently. A cagey politician once said, "Some of my friends are for it and some are against it – and I'm for my friends." In other words, I am not quite sure who is right about whether or not this was indeed a Christophany.

It is also interesting to note that in verse 18 of the passage we are about to study, we find the first use of the word *priest* in the Bible. The word *priest*, and the concept of priesthood, is one of the great themes that runs through the whole of Scripture. As a general principle, the first time a concept is introduced in the Bible, that first presentation makes it the seed of all subsequent truth that will come out of that concept. I believe this is particularly true of the first use here of the word *priest*.

You might ask, "Why are you introducing the theme of Communion with this passage?" I want to point out to you that in this encounter between Melchizedek and Abram, Melchizedek presented to Abram the very same emblems that are at the centre of every Communion service observed today – the bread and the wine.

Salem vs. Sodom

With that brief background, let's direct our attention now to the text in Genesis 14. Abram had just rescued his nephew Lot and Lot's family, recovering all the people and all the possessions which had been carried off during a battle. The attack had come from a military alliance of kings who invaded Sodom. Abram and his men had overcome the Kings of Sodom and Gomorrah, who fled the scene of the battle in defeat.

We pick up the story beginning at verse 17:

Then after his [Abram's] *return from the defeat at Chedorlaomer and the kings who were with him, the king of Sodom went out to meet him* [Abram] *at the valley of Shaveh (that is, the King's*

Valley). And Melchizedek king of Salem brought out bread and wine; now he was a priest of God Most High.

Genesis 14:17–18

I want you to notice that at this crucial moment of success, Abram was met by two kings: the King of Salem, Melchizedek, and the King of Sodom. These were kings over two cities with very different connotations and very different destinies. As the scene unfolds, we find that Abram was suddenly confronted with a choice. In a certain sense, he had to choose between these two kings.

Let's read verse 18 again and continue from there:

And Melchizedek king of Salem brought out bread and wine; now he was a priest of God Most High. He [Melchizedek] blessed him [Abram] and said, "Blessed be Abram of God Most High, Possessor of heaven and earth; And blessed be God Most High, Who has delivered your enemies into your hand." He [Abram] gave him [Melchizedek] a tenth [or a tithe] of all. The king of Sodom said to

Abram, "Give the people to me and take the goods for yourself."

verses 18–21

In other words, the King of Sodom was saying, "You have rescued me and all my people and all my possessions. Obviously, you want something for it. I'll be content if you just let me keep my people. As for me, I'll give you all the spoil that you've taken."

Abram said to the king of Sodom, "I have sworn to the Lord God Most High, possessor of heaven and earth, that I will not take a thread or a sandal thong or anything that is yours, for fear you would say, 'I have made Abram rich.' I will take nothing except what the young men have eaten, and the share of the men who went with me, Aner, Eshcol, and Mamre; let them take their share."

verses 22–24

In a very firm way, Abram said to the King of Sodom, "I don't want anything from you at all." He refused what the King of Sodom offered him. Instead, he accepted what Melchizedek offered. This is a brief glimpse of a principle I will develop later, because we too will have to make that choice. For now, I would like to take a closer look at the other king in our story – Melchizedek, King of Salem and priest of God Most High.

CHAPTER TWO

A Priest Forever

We have begun this book on Communion with the fascinating encounter between Abram and Melchizedek, the enigmatic Old Testament figure believed by many to have been a pre-incarnation manifestation of Jesus Christ. In Genesis 14:18 he is called "priest of God Most High." As I pointed out, it is very significant that this is the very first place where the word *priest* and the concept of *priesthood* is introduced in the Bible.

So far, we have actually learned very little about Melchizedek from the account in Genesis we just cited. However, the seventh chapter of Hebrews in the New Testament expounds upon the unique nature of Melchizedek's priesthood. Most importantly, it affirms that Jesus is a priest – not after the order of Levi, but after the order of Melchizedek.

Hebrews 7:17 states this clearly: *"For it is attested of Him* [Jesus], 'YOU ARE A PRIEST FOREVER ACCORDING TO THE ORDER

OF MELCHIZEDEK.'" This is actually a quote of David's prophetic statement in Psalm 110:4: "The LORD has sworn and will not change His mind, 'You are a priest forever according to the order of Melchizedek.'"

Two Separate Priesthoods

The writer of Hebrews draws a number of clear distinctions between the priesthood of Melchizedek and the priesthood of Levi. However, what I want to emphasise in this section is that the priesthood of Melchizedek was the initial priesthood, the archetype of all priesthoods. It was a superior priesthood. The priesthood of Levi, introduced 500 years later under the Law of Moses, was an inferior priesthood.

Interestingly enough, if you study the regulations of the Levitical priesthood, you will find that the Levitical priests never had anything to offer to God's people which God's people had not first offered to them. But Melchizedek offered to Abram that which Abram had never offered to Melchizedek – bread and wine.

We find another contrast of priesthoods in the sense that the Levitical priests could only continue in their priestly office for the length of their human lifetime. Hebrews 7:23 states it this way: "The former priests, on the one hand, existed in greater numbers because they were prevented by death from continuing."

You see, the law required a continual succession of priests, offering the same sacrifices over and over, year after year. They performed this service for themselves and for the people – offering up sacrifices which never completely dealt with the issue of sin.

However, Hebrews 7:26–27 describes a superior priesthood:

"For it was fitting for us to have such a high priest, holy, innocent, undefiled, separated from sinners and exalted above the heavens; who does not need daily, like those high priests, to offer up sacrifices, first for His own sins and then for the sins of the people, because He did this once for all when He offered up Himself.

One Eternal Sacrifice

When speaking about Jesus as a High Priest after the order of Melchizedek, the writer of Hebrews says that this Man, after He had offered one sacrifice for sin forever, sat down at the right hand of the Most High God.

Now the main point in what has been said is this: we have such a high priest, who has taken His seat at the right hand of the throne of the Majesty in the heavens.

Hebrews 8:1

Levitical priests always stood; they never sat. Jesus, however, was a priest after the order of Melchizedek. After He had offered the sacrifice of Himself on the cross, He sat down. Do you see the contrast? They stood; He sat.

What does this mean? The Levitical priests stood because their task was never complete; they could never offer the last sacrifice. In contrast, Jesus sat – because He offered one sacrifice for sin forever. He was never going to have to offer any sacrifice again.

We see, therefore, that the Levitical position was a temporary priesthood. But Jesus' position is an eternal priesthood. They offered many sacrifices for sin which never conclusively dealt with the sin issue. But Jesus offered one sacrifice for sin which dealt with sin forever and never had to be repeated. They stood. But Jesus sat – and He offered that which they had never offered to Him.

Let's continue to give our attention to the striking difference between the Levitical priesthood and their offering and the once-for-all sacrifice Jesus offered by virtue of His eternal priesthood.

CHAPTER THREE

A Profound Communion

In this brief chapter I hope to tie together the story of Communion in the New Testament with what we have been uncovering through the scriptures we have examined so far. We began our study in Genesis 14, where Abram encounters Melchizedek, "priest of God Most High." We then briefly picked up this thread in the Psalms, where David refers to that encounter in eternal, Messianic terms: "You are a Priest forever according to the order of Melchizedek" (Psalm 110:4). Then we looked at how the writer of Hebrews interpreted this eternal priesthood of Melchizedek for the Jewish believers, who had only ever known the priesthood of Levi.

Having laid this groundwork, it would be good for us to direct our attention to Matthew 26 – the description of the Lord's Supper. My hope, in light of what I have shared thus far, is that some life-changing truths will immediately become obvious to you. We will read Matthew 26, verses 26–29, which describe the scene at the Last Supper in which Jesus instituted the Eucharist. Regardless of the name you prefer to use for this event – the Lord's Table, the Last Supper, or Communion – these verses portray one of the most profound moments in all of Scripture.

While they were eating, Jesus took some bread, and after a blessing [or having blessed it, or having given thanks], *He broke it and gave it to the disciples, and said, "Take, eat; this is My body." And when He had taken a cup and given thanks, He gave it to them, saying, "Drink from it, all of you; for this is My blood of the covenant, which is poured out for many for forgiveness of sins. But I say to you, I will not drink of this fruit of the vine from now on until that day when I drink it new with you in My Father's kingdom."*

Matthew 26:26–29

The Reappearing of the First Priesthood

What was the meaning of Jesus taking the bread and then the wine and offering these elements to His disciples? What was He saying to them? He was saying, "In Me you see the priesthood of Melchizedek reappearing. It has been held in abeyance during the period when the Law was the covenant. Now, in the New Covenant, the priesthood of Melchizedek is being restored."

Interestingly enough, as I have pointed out earlier, Melchizedek was both a king and a priest. Under the Law of Moses, however, kingship and priesthood were separated – and they could not be united. This was because the priests had to come from the tribe of Levi and the king was required to come from the tribe of Judah. A king could never be a priest – and a priest could never be a king. This distinction is yet another indication of the inferiority of the Levitical priesthood.

However, everything changed when Jesus stood up at the Last Supper and brought forth the bread and the wine. He was saying, by that act, "Here is the priesthood of Melchizedek, which has been, as it were, held in suspension during the period of the Law of Moses. It is now reinstated in Me. I am a priest – not after the order of Levi – but after the order of Melchizedek."

Through that act of bringing forth the bread and the wine at the Last Supper, Jesus instituted the New Covenant in His blood. As He took the cup, He said, "This is the covenant of My blood which is to be shed on behalf of many for the forgiveness of sins."

This, then, is the background from Scripture of the Lord's Supper. It is a reinstatement of the priesthood of Melchizedek – the highest priesthood, the original priesthood. Furthermore, the emblems Jesus offered to His disciples were the same that Melchizedek had offered to Abram. Through Communion, Jesus reinstated the priesthood of Melchizedek – as well as the sacred elements we use in celebrating the Lord's Supper. In the chapters that follow, we will discover the significance of that reinstatement.

CHAPTER FOUR

The Seven Aspects of Communion

In the book of Genesis, the encounter between Abram and Melchizedek revealed a brief, prophetic glimpse of God's marvellous plan for our redemption. The bread and wine Melchizedek offered to Abram were a foreshadowing of the sacrament of Communion, which Jesus instituted two thousand years later in the Upper Room on the night before His crucifixion. These were the emblems of the crucifixion: the bread, His body; the wine, His blood. With these emblems, Jesus enacted the New Covenant in His blood, and He re-instituted the priesthood of Melchizedek. On that night of the Last Supper, our Savior gave us a beautiful, solemn sacrament, instructing us with these words: "Do this often, in remembrance of Me."

What does the New Testament teach us about our participation in this Communion? I believe the Bible reveals seven aspects of

Communion: three that speak of our relationship to Christ, three that speak of our relationship to Christ's body, and one that speaks of our relationship to the world. These seven aspects will be the focus of the succeeding chapters of this book.

Before we begin that segment of our study, I want to highlight two principles from chapters 10 and 11 of 1 Corinthians. These scripture passages will provide the basis for the discussion that will follow.

Sharing and Participating

We will start with First Corinthians 10, beginning at verse 14. Bear in mind that the issue Paul addressed here pertained to the type of food the Christians at Corinth could permit themselves to eat. Here was the question: could Christians eat food that was sold in the "shambles" – the temple slaughterhouses? Was it permissible for them to consume food which had initially been offered in sacrifice to pagan idols in pagan temples? That was the issue – and in connection with this issue Paul presents some lessons for us about the Lord's Supper.

Therefore, my beloved, flee from idolatry. I speak as to wise men; you judge what I say. Is not the cup of blessing which we bless a sharing in the blood of Christ? Is not the bread which we break a sharing in the body of Christ?

1 Corinthians 10:14–16

The word that is translated "sharing" here is the Greek word *koinonia*, which is normally translated as "fellowship." In the King James version, this word is translated "communion" – which means "having something together in common." So when we partake of the bread and the cup, we are affirming something that we all share – something we all have together in common with all other believers.

Since there is one bread, we who are many are one body; for we all partake of the one bread.

verse 17

Another facet of Communion is that we all partake of Christ's body. We all have a personal share in Christ's body – and we also share Christ's body with one another.

What do I mean then? That a thing sacrificed to idols is anything, or that an

29

idol is anything? No, but I say that the things which the Gentiles sacrifice, they sacrifice to demons and not to God; and I do not want you to become sharers in demons. You cannot drink the cup of the Lord and the cup of demons; . . .

verses 19–21

In other words, the food and drink in question here were a form of demon worship, because these pagan idols were demonic idols. The food being sold in the temple slaughterhouses had been sacrificed to demons.

Melchizedek or Sodom?

Connecting these verses from 1 Corinthians with our Genesis passage on Communion, we see that this was the same issue which confronted Abram. When Melchizedek met Abram in the King's Valley, Abram had to choose between what Melchizedek was offering and what the King of Sodom was offering. Somehow his conscience told him he could not partake from both. And neither can we.

Let's finish our examination of 1 Corinthians 10 by citing verse 21 again, to the end of verse 22.

You cannot drink the cup of the Lord and the cup of demons; you cannot partake of the table of the Lord and of the table of demons. Or do we provoke the Lord to jealousy? We are not stronger than He, are we?

verses 21–22

As we shall see at the conclusion of this book, we must be aware that our participation in Communion is separate and distinct from any other worldly activity.

Approaching the Lord's Table

The second passage I want to briefly examine before we cover the seven aspects of Communion is found in the next chapter of 1 Corinthians, chapter 11. The issue Paul addressed here was also quite a serious one: how we approach the Lord's Table. Let's begin at verse 23:

For I received from the Lord that which also I delivered to you, that the Lord Jesus in the night in which He was betrayed took bread; and when He had given thanks, He broke it and said, "This is My body, which is for you; do this in remembrance of Me." In the same way He took the cup also after supper, saying, "This cup is the new covenant in My blood; do this, as often as you drink it, in remembrance of Me." For as often as you eat this bread and drink the cup, you proclaim the Lord's death until He comes. Therefore whoever eats the bread or drinks the cup of the Lord in an unworthy manner, shall be guilty of the body and the blood of the Lord.

1 Corinthians 11:23–27

I regularly translate the word *guilty* in the last line of this passage as *responsible for* or *answerable for*. Once we have partaken of this Communion service, we have made it very clear that we know the teaching of the New Testament. What are the basic points of that teaching? Jesus, on the cross, died for our sins and shed His blood for our redemption. From the moment we take Communion onwards, we are answerable for what we know.

In that context, we continue now with verse 28 and 29:

But a man must examine himself, and in so doing he is to eat of the bread and drink of the cup. For he who eats and drinks, eats and drinks judgment to himself if he does not judge the body rightly.

Let's take a moment to look at the word judge at the end of verse 29: ". . . if he does not judge the body rightly." The King James Version and the New International Version use the words *discern* and *discerning*. I prefer both of those choices to the word judge. Let's substitute *discern* in verse 29 for the word *judge*.

For he who eats and drinks, eats and drinks judgment to himself if he does not discern the body rightly.

The same root word for *discern* is used when the New Testament refers to the gift of discerning of spirits. As I understand this concept in its New Testament use, the word means to see below the surface and see the inner spiritual reality. Perhaps *discern* remains the best word for our understanding of this passage.

Continuing on, we see that both verses 29 and 30 make very important points:

For he who eats and drinks, eats and drinks judgment to himself if he does not

*discern the body rightly. For this reason
many among you are weak and sick, and
a number sleep.*

That phrase, "a number sleep," means "a
number have died prematurely." Do you realise
that it is possible to die before your time? This
passage shows us the seriousness, the sanctity,
and the solemnity of the Lord's Table. As I said
earlier, these are very important verses. If we
partake wrongly, it can be a cause of sickness
and even of premature death.

How We Partake

By background, I am an Anglican. In a
certain sense, some of the teaching of the
Anglican Church would almost make salvation
hinge on Communion itself. But that is not the
complete truth. It depends on *how you partake*
of Communion. Far from being the means of
salvation, it can be the very opposite. It can
actually be the means of judgment. Therefore,
we must be careful not to base our concept of
our relationship with God merely on partaking
of Communion. It depends whether we partake
of it rightly or wrongly. This, as we said, is a
very serious issue.

Let's finish our preface to the seven aspects of Communion by examining verses 31 and 32:

But if we judged ourselves rightly, we would not be judged. But when we are judged, we are disciplined by the Lord so that we will not be condemned along with the world.

Can you see that the Lord is doing everything He can possibly do for us in this situation? First of all, He says, "If you will judge yourself and so partake in a worthy manner, I won't have to discipline you." Then He says, "If you fail to judge yourself, then I will have to discipline you. But even if I discipline you, that is better than being judged with the world." Judgment with the world is the ultimate disaster that we need to avoid.

Having studied these passages in 1 Corinthians 10 and 11, we are now ready to move on to the next part of our study: the seven main aspects of Communion. It is my hope that these aspects will provide an even deeper understanding of how you and I relate to Jesus and His body when we are partaking in this beautiful and solemn sacrament of Communion.

CHAPTER FIVE

Aspect 1: Proclamation

At the beginning of the previous chapter, we asked this question: What does the New Testament teach us as Christians about our participation in the sacrament of Communion? In response to that question I stated that the Bible reveals seven main aspects, which I will present in a specific order. The first three pertain to our **relationship to Christ**. The next three pertain to our **relationship to Christ's body**. And the last one pertains to our relationship to the world.

In relation to Christ Jesus Himself, I believe that partaking of Communion has three aspects. First, *proclamation*; second, *remembrance*; and third, *anticipation*. In this brief chapter we will look at the first aspect, proclamation, by reading the words of Paul in 1 Corinthians 11:26:

For as often as you eat this bread and drink the cup, you proclaim the Lord's death until He comes.

Proclaiming to the Universe

This verse says it very simply. In partaking of Communion, we are proclaiming the death of the Lord. We are not merely proclaiming this truth to our fellow believers. In fact, I don't think that is the most important factor at all. Rather, we are proclaiming it to the world. Even more importantly, we are proclaiming the death of the Lord to the whole unseen realm. We are proclaiming to angels, both good and evil; to spirits, good and evil. We are proclaiming to the whole universe the death of Jesus Christ. It is an authoritative, powerful act of proclamation.

You may not be a preacher by ministry or calling. But when you partake of these emblems, you are making a proclamation of tremendous significance. You are proclaiming to the whole universe that Jesus Christ, the Son of God, died and shed His blood on your behalf to redeem you. You are proclaiming your faith in Him as Savior. You are proclaiming your faith in His atoning death on your behalf.

This, then, is the first aspect: Communion is *primarily* an act of proclamation. As Paul said in the verse we just read, "... you proclaim the Lord's death until He comes."

CHAPTER SIX

Aspect 2: Remembrance

The second aspect of Communion in relationship to Jesus is *remembrance*. When we take Communion, we look back to His death. Jesus Himself made the point about remembrance, as quoted by Paul in 1 Corinthians 11:25:

> *"This cup is the new covenant in My blood; do this, as often as you drink it, in remembrance of Me."*

Then Paul adds the aspect of remembering His death in verse 26: "For as often as you eat this bread and drink the cup, you proclaim the Lord's death until He comes."

Sacraments and Ordinances

To help us with *remembrance*, there are traditions in the Christian life. These are typically called sacraments or ordinances, depending on what your particular denominational background teaches. In essence, a sacrament or an ordinance is a presentation of the most important truths of the gospel. These truths are so significant that God, in His sovereign wisdom, has arranged a special way to emphasise them. Not only do we present them in words – we also present them in symbolical acts.

For five years of my life, I was a trainer of teachers for schools in east Africa. One of the concepts that we instilled in our trainee teachers was this principle: "Children remember forty percent of what they hear, sixty percent of what they hear and see, and eighty percent of what they hear, see, and do." The percentages may have changed over the years, but the principle remains the same. If you want to make maximum impact on a child's mind, go beyond merely letting a child hear a truth. Let the child hear it, see it, and do it. Let those children translate what they learn into an action that they themselves perform.

As I understand sacraments or ordinances, the same principle applies. The great basic truths of the New Testament are so important that God has ordained for us not merely to hear them, nor even merely hear and see them. Rather He insists that we hear them, see them, and do them.

Across the Body of Christ, there are various traditions as to the number of actual sacraments or ordinances taught in the New Testament. Space does not permit a presentation of all of them here. But for our purposes in this chapter I will briefly highlight three sacraments of the Church.

1. **Baptism.** The first of these sacraments is *baptism*. This is the initiatory sacrament or ordinance by which we become publicly identified with Christ and His body. It is an act. No matter how it is performed – whether by sprinkling or by immersion – the basic teaching regarding baptism shared by all main Christian churches is the same. It is a public act of identification with the Lord Jesus Christ in His death, burial and resurrection.

Here is my personal belief. Without that act of identification, a believer has no right to claim a place in the body of Christ. There is not one instance in the New Testament of anybody claiming salvation without being baptised. You cannot find one. In Mark 16:16, Jesus said, "He who has believed and has been baptised shall be saved." This sacrament is of such importance – our identification with Jesus in death, burial and resurrection – that God has ordained it for all believers. Every time a person is admitted to the body of Christ, they shall confirm that entrance with this symbolic action. Not only that, but all those who witness this baptism are themselves reminded of its importance.

2. **Anointing the sick.** Another ordinance or sacrament is the *anointing of the sick* with oil. This truth is so important that God doesn't let us merely hear it, or hear it and see it, but He enables us to act it out.

What is the significance of anointing the sick with oil? Throughout the Scripture, the oil always typifies the Holy Spirit. When we anoint the sick with oil, we are declaring to the whole universe that we believe the Holy Spirit will do what the Scripture says He will do. He will quicken; He will give life; and He will restore health to the body of the sick believer.

3. **Communion.** The third sacrament or ordinance is the ordinance of *Communion, the Eucharist*, or *the Lord's Supper*. In this sacrament, we are declaring that Jesus Christ, the Son of God, died and shed His blood on the cross for us. Every time you and I do this, we do it in remembrance of Him. God never

wants us to forget the fact that Jesus died for us as sinners.

I am convinced that a lot of Christians go through much spiritual trouble because their minds are not focused on the death of Jesus. They say, "I wonder if God loves me. Has God forgotten me?" You could not talk like that if you remembered the cross. The cross is the ultimate demonstration of God's love for each of us.

Hear again the words in Romans 8:32:

He who did not spare His own Son, but delivered Him over for us all, how will He not also with Him freely give us all things?

This is the guarantee that the total inheritance is ours. God is saying, "It is so important – especially in times of darkness, testing and pressure – that my people enact this sacrament and this ordinance. By taking the Lord's Supper, you will continually remember the fact of Jesus' death and sacrifice for you." God is saying to us, "I never want you to forget it. I want you to be continually reminded of it."

Take Communion Often

In the King James Version, 1 Corinthians 11:25 says that when Jesus took the cup, He said, "This do ye, as oft as ye drink it, in remembrance of me." Some critics of certain cross sections of the Protestant Church have said, "We have changed that to 'as seldom as ye drink it.'"

I have become absolutely convinced that believers should be regularly remembering the Lord's death. Some of the churches I associated with didn't observe Communion often enough. What I am about to say next may either shock you or bless you, but Ruth and I decided to take the Lord's Supper together every morning. I don't ever want to forget Communion.

It is said that Smith Wigglesworth, one of the great pioneer evangelists of the Pentecostal movement, wanted to take Communion wherever he could get it. During his evangelistic travels, he literally went looking for any church having a Communion service. When he found one, he went in and shared in that sacrament. I truly believe that many of our problems – spiritual, emotional, psychological – are due to the fact we don't remember the Lord's death often enough.

CHAPTER SEVEN

Aspect 3: Anticipation

The third aspect of Communion in relationship to Jesus is *anticipation*. It is very closely connected to the first two: *proclamation* and *remembrance*. We will reference 1 Corinthians 11:26 once again – this time paying close attention to the ending:

> *For as often as you eat this bread and drink the cup, you proclaim the Lord's death* [but not forever] *until He comes.*

We do not merely look back to His death and proclaim it. Rather, we also look forward to His coming! Every time we observe this ordinance together, we are reminding ourselves of these two truths: first of all, that Jesus died on the cross for our sins; secondly, that He is coming again!

If you and I could really live – moment to moment – in the consciousness that Jesus died for you and me in the past and that He is coming for you and me in the future, many of our bouts of depression and dark moods would never arise.

This assertion was beautifully expressed by an old saint of past generations, Sir Robert Anderson, in a book he wrote called *The Coming Prince*. In that book, he said that when we partake of Communion, everything else drops out of sight. For that time, we focus only on the issues that really matter. This is the way Anderson put it: "No past but the cross; no future but the coming."

How good it is when we let all the incidental, minor matters that trouble, perplex and confuse us fade out of sight for a little while. We look back to the cross – and then we look forward to the coming.

Come Quickly, Lord Jesus!

There were periods in past revivals and renewals when Christians were very conscious of the coming of the Lord. Even their conversation was marked with an expectancy – as if the Lord was coming within the next five years. But then, He didn't come. As a result, we have seen the wrong kind of reaction: "Well, it's foolish to talk about the Lord's coming."

However, as far as I am concerned, it is *not* foolish to talk about the Lord's coming. I believe the Lord is coming, and I believe He is coming quickly. I believe He is coming suddenly. The New Testament ends with this prayer: "He who testifies to these things says, 'Surely I am coming quickly.' Amen. Even so, come, Lord Jesus!" (Revelation 22:20 NKJV).

I think there is something wrong with our spiritual condition if we can't pray that prayer with a sincere heart. Those words were written about twenty centuries ago. Was it silly to pray them then? Not as far as I am concerned.

No matter what we do as the Body of Christ (and we have great responsibilities on earth which we have not yet discharged), I am convinced that the only ultimate solution to earth's problems is the personal return of Jesus. If He doesn't come back, we are in a mess we will never get out of.

The Coming Prince

With the conclusion of this chapter, we have examined the first three aspects of our participation in Communion. Let me just repeat those three aspects in our relationship to Christ. First, *proclamation*; second, *remembrance*, looking back to the past; third, *anticipation*; looking forward to the future.

Why don't we close this section of our study by repeating those words of Sir Robert Anderson which beautifully summarise this chapter? (Perhaps you would like to read them out loud, as a proclamation of your own.)

Let's repeat them three times:

"No past but the cross; no future but the coming."

"No past but the cross; no future but the coming."

"No past but the cross; no future but the coming."

CHAPTER EIGHT

Aspect 4: Recognition

In this and the following two chapters we will begin our examination of the next three aspects of Communion – aspects four, five and six. When we are observing the Table of the Lord, these aspects speak to our relationship to Christ's body. The three words I have chosen for these aspects are *recognition, participation* and *sharing*.

In this chapter, the aspect we will focus upon is recognition. Let's begin by taking another look at a verse previously examined in this study, 1 Corinthians 11:29:

For he who eats and drinks, eats and drinks judgment to himself if he does not judge [or discern] *the body rightly.*

You may remember our discussion about replacing the word *judge* with the word *discern*, which is used in other Bible versions. In regard to the fourth aspect, *recognition*, I believe this verse has two very important applications for us personally. Perhaps the word *discern* will help us to see those applications more clearly.

Seeing Below the Surface

From time to time during my years in the ministry of deliverance, the Lord gave me the gift of the discerning of spirits. When this gift operated, it was as if I could see below the surface of the personality of the brother or sister seeking help. I was able to perceive something in the inner spiritual condition of the person needing ministry – something beyond what could be revealed to the natural senses. I could, in a sense, *recognise* the inner reality. Many times, I have discerned in people the spirit of death operating in them. I cannot exactly tell you how, but I knew it when I saw it – as if I were looking deep into their spirit.

During Communion, I believe that is how we should see the bread – the element representing Christ's body. First, we look at the bread and we see just plain bread. Some people, such as myself, prefer to take Passover matzo. Other people in certain church traditions take wafers. I remember as a young boy growing up in the Anglican Church partaking of wafers.

Unleavened bread is obviously what Jesus and His disciples partook of, because it was the Passover and they were not allowed to eat anything with leaven. For us, whether it is a wafer, a piece of matzo, unleavened bread, or just a piece of ordinary baked bread, we can discern its greater significance. If we exercise discernment, we will recognise the reality below the surface. What will we see? We will see the body of the Lord.

Two Applications

I personally believe that when I partake of Communion, having met God's conditions, then that piece of bread I am feeding upon is the body of the Lord. I am not doing something symbolic; I am doing something real. It is not just a symbol; it is the Lord's body. That is discerning. That is the first application of "discerning the body rightly."

Paul says, however, that because it is one loaf, we are one body. So not merely does the loaf represent and become for me the body of the Lord that I partake of and feed upon. It also represents to me the collective body of the Lord – the Church, which is His body. This is the second application of the scripture "discerning the body rightly." Once again, my friend, you and I need discernment to understand these important concepts.

My friend, Bob Mumford, would regularly say, "The Lord has got a lot of strange kids!" In the natural, you could look at the person next to you in a Communion service and say, "I don't see much to get excited about!" Or, you could look in the mirror and perhaps say the same about yourself.

But when we are observing the Lord's Supper, you and I are supposed to see below the surface. When I look at my brother or my sister in the pew beside me or in front of me, I don't see just a person – I see a member of the body of Christ. I see someone for whom Jesus died and shed His blood.

I must realise at such a point that if I don't appreciate and honour that person, I am grieving the heart of the Lord. Why? Because the Lord loves that dear saint sitting next to me enough to die for that person. It cannot but grieve the Lord bitterly if we have a wrong, depreciatory attitude towards a member of His body.

Caring for Each Other

I believe this was the real problem of the Corinthians. There were many wrong relationships between them. They didn't discern –

or recognise – the Lord's body in one another. Consequently, Paul said to them, "For this reason many among you are weak and sick, and a number sleep [have even died]" (1 Corinthians 11:30). Could this be one major cause of sickness among Christians today? It may well be, because many Christians do not treat one another the least bit like members of Christ's body. I say that with deep regret.

The truth is, we have all been mistreated. At times, when painful events have happened to me as a result of a fellow believer's actions, I have felt like saying, "With friends like that, I don't need enemies." And yet, I don't believe that I have suffered any worse than others. In fact, on the whole, I think many others have suffered worse than I have.

So this aspect of Communion, *recognition*, is about discernment. It is about looking below the outward and recognising the inner reality – the permanent, the spiritual, and the eternal.

There are two applications of this aspect. First of all, in that little piece of bread in your hand is the very body of the Lord, if you partake rightly. Second, residing in the people around you who partake of the same bread is the living body of the Lord. They are the members of His body. Let us pray that we will discern one another rightly.

Paul brings up another important consideration in the following verse: "But a man must examine himself, and in so doing he is to eat of the bread and drink of the cup" (1 Corinthians 11:28).

I am so glad I don't have to examine other people. In fact, the truth is this: I have a full time job examining myself!

CHAPTER NINE

Aspect 5: Participation

The next aspect of Communion in relationship to Christ's body is *participation*. To begin this section, we will look again at 1 Corinthians 10:17:

Since there is one bread, we who are many are one body; for we all partake of the one bread.

When we *partake* (a verb) of the bread, that is our *participation* (a noun) in Communion. We are partakers. In connection to that, I would like to examine John 6:53–58:

So Jesus said to them, "Truly, truly I say to you, unless you eat the flesh of the Son of Man and drink His blood, you have no life in yourselves."

verse 53

Here is the point of this verse: there is only one source of life. It is in the flesh and the blood of the Lord.

At one time, I lived in an Arab community in what was then Palestine, now known as

Israel. I lived in a town called Ramallah. During my time in Ramallah, I discovered that when Arab believers take the Lord's Supper, they actually say (in Arabic), "We want to drink the blood of Jesus." That is the actual phrase they use. Actually, I think it is very appropriate.

Of course, there is something in every human being that recoils at the thought of feeding upon the flesh and drinking the blood of the Lord. That factor was certainly present with the disciples. When Jesus said these words in John 6, some of His disciples left Him. They said, "We can't take that kind of talk." In contrast to that reaction, I have taught myself for many years to *humble* myself before the Word of God, not to *argue* with it. Jesus said, "Unless you eat My flesh and drink My blood you have no life." That statement is true. That settles it. When Jesus has said something like this, He has the last word in the matter.

Resurrection

Let's continue with our study of John 6, citing verse 54:

"He who eats My flesh and drinks My blood has eternal life and I will raise him up on the last day."

I don't know whether or not you can receive what I am about to say, but I have spent a lot of time researching and meditating on the topic of resurrection. In fact, I wrote a book called *Resurrection of the Body*. Like all orthodox Christians of all ages, I believe in the resurrection of the body as part of the Apostles' Creed. I don't believe God is going to give us a different body, or some other body. He is going to give us back *the same body*, in a glorified state. Do you believe that? If you don't, you need to read what is said in your Bible.

How is the Lord going to gather together all the scattered remnants of a body that has been dead for centuries? Ultimately, you may have to direct that question to the Lord. But I simply believe He is going to do it.

If I am right, it seems to me that what the Lord is saying in this verse is something like this: "When you partake of the bread and of the cup in faith, meeting the conditions, something happens to your physical body that guarantees that I will resurrect it."

We Will be Changed

This is what I believe. When you take Communion in faith, from then on your body is different from the body of a person who has never partaken of the body and blood of the Lord. There will be a moment when the Lord commands the archangel Gabriel to sound the trumpet – when He gives the shout that will arouse the dead in Christ. In that moment, all those little parts of your body – no matter where or when they were scattered – will jump together and form themselves into one. You will come forth with a new, glorified body; new in the sense of being glorified – but the same in the sense of having the same constituent parts that your body had when it was still alive. As I see it, the guarantee of resurrection is partaking of the body and the blood of the Lord. As that verse, in John 6:54, says:

"He who eats My flesh and drinks My blood has eternal life ..."

Please note, my friend. It does not say *will* have, but has.

". . . and I will raise him up on the last day."

That is a guarantee spoken to us directly by Jesus.

Facing Sorrows

When my first wife, Lydia, was called home by the Lord, it was the hardest and bitterest event that ever happened in my Christian experience. I want to tell you, my dear friend, death is very real. It is not pretty. It is cruel. Any religion that does not have an answer to death does not meet the needs of humanity. The only religion that has such an answer is Christianity.

When Lydia was called home, I had been a preacher for more than thirty years. At that difficult moment, I had to sit down and say to myself, "Do I believe what I have been preaching? I have preached that there will be a resurrection – that there will be a reunion. Do I believe it?" I thought it over sombrely, carefully. Then I said to myself, "Yes, I believe it." If I didn't believe it, I would ultimately be a hopeless person.

When believers in Christ who are near and dear to us die, we grieve – not as the world sorrows, because the world sorrows without hope. But we have hope. We, the righteous, have hope in His death.

Losing a mate is different from any other experience in life. It is like having your own flesh and blood torn from you. There is nothing that can take us through such an experience as that except this message. The more often we partake of Communion, the deeper our peace will be when life's crises come.

Our Life Source

Let's continue our study of John chapter 6, focusing on verses 55 and 56:

"For My flesh is true food and My blood is true drink. He who eats My flesh and drinks My blood abides in Me, and I in him."

verse 55–56

What Jesus says here could be translated as a continuous present: "He who *goes on eating* My flesh *and drinking* My blood *goes on abiding* in Me and I in him."

"As the living Father sent Me, and I live because of the Father, so he who eats Me, he also will live because of Me."

verse 57

The King James Version says it this way:

*"As the living Father hath sent me, and I
live by the Father: so he that eateth me,
even he shall live by me."*

John 6:57 KJV

In a way, I prefer that version. Jesus lived a
life of total dependence on the life of the Father.
The Father was His life source. Incidentally,
when Jesus became totally identified with our
sin, and He was consequently cut off from that
life source, He died.

Just as God the Father is the life source of
Jesus the Son, Jesus is the life source of every
true believer. As Jesus lived by the Father, so
we live by Him. Our life is dependent on our
continuing relationship with Him.

In verse 58 of John 6, Jesus says that when
we partake of these emblems, we are partaking
of the life source.

*"This is the bread which came down out
of heaven; not as the fathers ate and died;
he who eats this bread will live forever."*

verse 58

Do you know what is the most exciting part
about those words? They are true. Do you know
what always blesses me about the Bible? Most

of the really important truths are said in words of one syllable: "He – who – eats – this – bread – will – live . . . forever." That is what Jesus promises. It is true.

CHAPTER TEN

Aspect 6: Sharing

In the previous two chapters we have been discussing how we relate to Christ's body when we partake of Communion. First, we looked at *recognition*. We saw that it requires discernment to see that the bread and wine of which we have partaken is the actual body of Jesus – in us and in our fellow believers. Next, we focused on *participation*. We saw that partaking of His flesh and blood enables us to live forever in Him. In this chapter we will discuss aspect 6, the next aspect of relating to Christ's body in Communion, which is *sharing* in Communion with others.

Our text for the first point we will make in this matter of sharing is 1 Corinthians 10:16:

Is not the cup of blessing which we bless a sharing in the blood of Christ? Is not the bread which we break a sharing in the body of Christ?

When we partake of the bread and the cup, we are sharing in the body of Christ. We are sharing with all our fellow believers. It is a reminder to us that we are part of a vast company.

We may be just a tiny little group, insignificant in our own eyes and situation. But when we share in Communion, recognising the immense spiritual reality of that principle, we realise the truth. We are part of a group of people who started in the New Testament, have gone on ever since, and are continuing on still.

Sharing Across the Veil

When I teach on Communion, I am often reminded of my Anglican heritage. I remember that in the Anglican Church, we used to celebrate something called All Saints' Day. I am sorry to say that when I became a Pentecostal, I forgot all about All Saints' Day.

However, all that forgetfulness changed when my wife, Lydia, was called home by the Lord. For the first time in my life, I couldn't keep my preaching commitments. The only other occasion on which I had ever reneged on a preaching commitment was when I was sick. However, for two or three weeks after Lydia's death, I just told people, "I'm sorry, but I am not ready to preach."

But then I realised that my refusal to preach would not have pleased Lydia the least bit! Why should I sit at home? If she were here she would want me to be out preaching! So I went to the next commitment I had.

That commitment was the Southeast Charismatic Catholic Fellowship, held in Augusta, Georgia. Of course, it was primarily a Catholic gathering. Do you know what I discovered upon my arrival? It was All Saints' Day. And do you know what they were celebrating? Communion – with the whole body of Christ. Not just with those on earth, but with those who had gone before them.

That was the first public meeting in which I participated after Lydia's death. Nothing could have been more appropriate. I suddenly got a glimpse of a truth which I ought to have known all along. What I saw was this: the veil that separates believers between this world and the next is not dark and heavy – it is a very fine, gauzy veil. The dark and heavy veil is in this world – between those who believe and those who don't.

Lydia's Danish Roots

I would like to tell a few more anecdotes about Lydia to take us to the end of this chapter. These personal stories are relevant examples of the aspect we are discussing: sharing in Communion.

It may be possible that you knew Lydia personally, or made her acquaintance at some time. I would have to say she was the bravest person I ever met. Lydia was a very forthright person. She never said anything without purpose. In all the years we lived together, I never heard her say something she didn't mean. She was Danish. If you know European culture, the most outspoken people in Europe are the Danes. And the most outspoken Dane was Lydia!

As you might suspect, it took some adjusting on my part to get used to living with such an outspoken person. She used to say to me, "You British are a nation of diplomats. Nobody ever knows when you really mean what you say." It took a little while to digest that, but it was absolutely correct.

I'll try here to be careful in how I express this, but Lydia came out of the Lutheran Church in Denmark. She was one of the pioneers of the Pentecostal movement in her nation. At the age of 38, she came into the baptism in the Holy Spirit without really knowing what had happened to her. In her desire to obey the Scriptures, she then accepted the challenge of being baptised as a believer by immersion. This act on Lydia's part literally scandalised the whole Danish nation, which is not a large nation. (Incidentally, this story is told in the book about Lydia's life: *Appointment in Jerusalem*.)

In fact, her case went before the Danish Parliament as to whether she could continue as a teacher in a Danish state school after doing something so heretical as being "re-baptised" as a believer. (Re-baptism was the crux of the issue for the Lutherans.) Americans might have difficulty understanding that culture, but it was very real in Europe. For about fifty years, Lydia had a running war with the Lutheran Church. To introduce her to a Lutheran pastor was like dangling a red rag in front of a bull!

Light in the Darkness

About two years before Lydia died, a dear brother in the Lord asked if he could drop by to see us. At that time, Lydia was having very deep spiritual problems. She was even doubting her own salvation. I had read about this happening to men and women of God, but I didn't know it could happen to someone so close to me.

It just so happened that this visiting brother had a particular ministry in the area of the "word of knowledge." When praying with people, he would sometimes get a very vivid mental picture of the person's particular need, problem or situation. After the three of us prayed together for a while in our living room, I said to Tom, "Do you see anything?" He said, "Well, yes, I do. I see a large church building. It is rather empty. It has stained glass windows, and it has a choir stall."

Then he asked Lydia, "Would that have anything to do with you?"

Lydia replied, "Absolutely nothing."

"Wait a minute," I said to Tom. Then I asked him, "Do you think it could be a Lutheran church?"

He said, "Yes, that's the kind of church it is."

So I said to Lydia, "What do you think about the Lutheran church?"

She replied, "I hate them!"

I then said to my dear wife, "You cannot hate anybody. That is not permitted. You have to repent."

Repent she did – and that was the turning point. After that time together, she came out of the darkness into the light. God arranged that experience for her, because within two years He had taken her home.

Let me pause at this point to say this: if today you are in darkness, check on your attitudes and your relationships. Is there anybody you hate? Anybody you have not forgiven?

Communion with the Saints

This is not the end of the story. About a year after Lydia died, I was invited to speak at the Lutheran Charismatic Conference held every summer in Minneapolis. We had a glorious time. I had the privilege of teaching Bible classes to about nine thousand people for three days in succession.

The conference concluded with the whole congregation – maybe fourteen thousand persons in all – celebrating the Eucharist together. Since I was no longer on the platform, I was very happy to take my place in the auditorium as a member of the congregation, sitting in a pew with the other people. I preferred to have my communion with the Lord and His body in a very intimate and private way.

Anyhow, this was the situation as it took place – and I hope what I am about to share next won't disturb your theology. As I sat there partaking of Communion in a Lutheran Eucharist, for the first time ever – in a way that I had never in my life experienced before – I knew that I was partaking of the body and the blood of the Lord. I didn't just believe it. I *knew* it.

Here is what I would like to say now, and I hope you will receive it. While I was sitting there in that Lutheran congregation partaking of a Lutheran Eucharist, I had a communication from Lydia in glory. I don't know whether you believe in this or not. But this is what was communicated to me. I won't say Lydia spoke to me, but somehow what I sensed from her was, "I am glad you are here for my sake."

I saw, then, how tremendously appropriate it was. I was representing both Lydia and myself as I took that act of love, communion and reconciliation with my Lutheran brothers and sisters – not merely on my behalf, but on her behalf as well.

For me, after these experiences of sharing in the body of Christ, this aspect of Communion has become very real.

When we participate in a Communion service, all the saints who have gone before are sharing together with us in this commemoration of the Lord's death. For this one truth unites all believers from all ages, races, denominations, and backgrounds – the death and resurrection of the Lord Jesus Christ.

CHAPTER ELEVEN

Aspect 7: Separation

What should be our response and participation in Communion? That is the primary question we have sought to answer in this book. As I previously stated, the Scriptures reveal that when we are observing Communion, we are relating to Jesus Christ in seven ways, or aspects. Here is a brief summary of the first six aspects which we have already discussed:

1. **Proclamation:** *proclaiming His death to the seen and the unseen realms*

2. **Remembrance:** *remembering His death (He asked us to do so)*

3. **Anticipation:** *anticipating His return*

4. **Recognition:** *discerning the true nature of the bread and the cup, His body*

5. **Participation:** *participating in His death and resurrection by eating of His flesh and blood*

6. **Sharing:** *sharing in the Communion with all believers here and in eternity*

As you can see from this list, these six aspects focus on our relationship to Jesus Christ and all believers in Communion. The first three relate to Jesus Himself, and the next three relate to His body.

In this final chapter we will discuss the seventh aspect of Communion. This aspect is different from the first six because it is not about Communion in relationship to Jesus Christ. Rather, it focuses on Communion as it relates to the world – specifically, to unbelievers. The word I have chosen for the seventh aspect is *separation*.

Drawing the Line

Earlier in our study we read a passage from 1 Corinthians, chapter 10, where Paul was addressing a cultural issue in that church: was it permissible for a believer to eat meat that had been sacrificed to demon gods? I believe Paul's response to the Corinthian Church has application for us as well. Let's read 1 Corinthians 10, verses 20–21:

No, but I say that the things which the Gentiles sacrifice, they sacrifice to demons, and not to God; and I do not want you to become sharers in demons. You cannot drink the cup of the Lord and the cup of demons; you cannot partake of the table of the Lord and the table of demons.

To me, these verses mean that when we partake of Communion, we are drawing a line of separation between us and everything that is satanic in any shape or form. We are removing ourselves from every kind of occult involvement, every kind of activity that is not Christ-honouring. We cannot have a foot in both camps.

I endeavoured in my home to make sure that our family never retained any publication that dishonoured Jesus Christ. At the end of the seventh chapter of Deuteronomy, Moses said to the children of Israel, "And you shall not bring an abominable thing into your house, and become accursed like it" (Deuteronomy 7:26 RSV).

My dear friend, I would suggest that the next time you go home after partaking in the Eucharist or Communion, you might need to have a housecleaning. Don't retain any little images of Buddha. Don't retain any signs of the horoscope or the zodiac. Do you understand why? Those things are demonic – and you cannot partake of the table of the Lord and the table of demons. You cannot share the things of Satan and the things of the Lord.

You see, we are confronted with the same issue which confronted Abram. When Melchizedek met Abram in the King's Valley, Abram had to choose between what Melchizedek was offering and what the King of Sodom was offering. His conscience told him he could not partake from both. Nor can we.

No Mixture

In conclusion, I would like to read a passage from the book of Ezra, which particularly emphasises this last point. The fourth chapter of Ezra describes the rebuilding of the temple by the Jewish exiles, who had returned to Jerusalem from Babylon. We will look at only the first three verses. To me, they so clearly emphasise this issue of separation between those who are God's people and those who are not God's people.

Now when the enemies of Judah and Benjamin heard that the people of the exile were building a temple to the Lord God of Israel . . . [Please note, it was a temple to the one true God] . . . *they approached Zerubbabel and the heads of the fathers' households, and said to them, "Let us build with you, for we, like you, seek your God; and we have been sacrificing to Him since the days of Esar-haddon king of Assyria, who brought us up here."*

Ezra 4:1–2

At first blush, this might have sounded like a friendly offer. But if you know the historical background of those who were asking, these people had a very mixed form of worship. They had elements of the Mosaic Law and covenant. But they also had elements of heathenism and demonism, including child sacrifice.

When they saw God's people building God's house in Jerusalem, they said, "Let us join with you. We would like to be in on this project."

However, if you were to read the rest of the chapter, you would discover they were up to no good – which explains the following answer given to them by the Jewish leaders.

But Zerubbabel and Jeshua and the rest of the heads of the fathers' households of Israel said to them, "You have nothing in common with us in building a house to our God;. . ."

verse 3

If I might paraphrase what they were saying, it was something like this: "Don't you dare try to cross that line of separation. Your god and our God are not the same – even if you use some of the same language that we use."

We Ourselves Together

At the conclusion of this Ezra passage, we come to the verse I want to emphasise. We find it at the end of verse 3:

". . . but we ourselves will together build to the Lord God of Israel . . ."

To me, those three words sum up this message; "We ourselves together."

"We" speaks of plurality – all of God's people together.

"Ourselves" speaks of separation – only us and not you.

"Together" speaks of unity.

That is where we must be today in the body of Christ, His Church. Plurality – a body made up of many, many members; Separation – no compromise with satanic elements; and Unity – we will do it together.

CHAPTER TWELVE

Our Response to Communion

We have explored these seven aspects of Communion in great detail. Our goal has been to develop a deeper understanding of how you and I relate to Jesus, His body, and the world when we partake of this beautiful and solemn sacrament of Communion.

Now we return to the question we have asked throughout this book: what should be our response? Perhaps this book has moved you personally to place a greater emphasis on the observance of the Lord's Supper. In a moment we will voice a prayer together that expresses that commitment.

It may be that you find yourself in a similar dilemma as Lydia – carrying wounds that seem to be separating you from God. We saw from the incidents I related that for Lydia, repentance was the turning point. She came out of the darkness into the light. If today you are in darkness, you too can come into the light.

As you think about approaching the Lord's Table, are there any attitudes in your heart for which you need to repent? Is there anybody you hate? Anybody you have not forgiven? Are you struggling with God Himself? Those issues need to be resolved.

Why don't we deal with all these matters now in prayer together? Let's ask God to begin to prepare our hearts right now with the following prayer:

"Heavenly Father, how deeply grateful I am for this beautiful sacrament of Communion – given to us by Jesus the night before His crucifixion. I commit myself now to partake of this sacrament more often – as a powerful way of proclaiming Your death, remembering You, anticipating Your return, recognising Your body, participating in Your death and resurrection, sharing with all believers, and separating myself from worldly pursuits. Thank you that as I partake, I am receiving life from You and celebrating the eternal life You have brought to me.

I come out of darkness now into the light. I repent of my sins and attitudes. I ask for forgiveness through Jesus' sacrifice on the cross for me. In Jesus' name, I forgive all those who have hurt me, and I declare my trust in You and Your plans for my life.

I prepare my heart now to meet You at every opportunity I will have to partake of this wonderful sacrament of Holy Communion. Amen."

About the Author

Derek Prince (1915–2003) was born in India of British parents. Educated as a scholar of Greek and Latin at Eton College and Cambridge University, England, he held a Fellowship in Ancient and Modern Philosophy at King's College. He also studied several modern languages, including Hebrew and Aramaic, at Cambridge University and the Hebrew University in Jerusalem.

While serving with the British army in World War II, he began to study the Bible and experienced a life-changing encounter with Jesus Christ. Out of this encounter he formed two conclusions: first, that Jesus Christ is alive; second, that the Bible is a true, relevant, up-to-date book. These conclusions altered the whole course of his life, which he then devoted to studying and teaching the Bible.

Derek's main gift of explaining the Bible and its teaching in a clear and simple way has helped build a foundation of faith in millions of lives. His non-denominational, non-sectarian approach "Keys to Successful Living" has made his teaching equally relevant and helpful to people from all racial and religious backgrounds.

He is the author of over 50 books, 600 audio and 100 video teachings, many of which have been translated and published in more than 100 languages. His daily radio broadcast is translated into Arabic, Chinese (Amoy, Cantonese, Mandarin, Shanghainese, Swatow), Croatian, German, Malagasy, Mongolian, Russian, Samoan, Spanish and Tongan. The radio programme continues to touch lives around the world.

Derek Prince Ministries continues to reach out to believers in over 140 countries with Derek's teachings, fulfilling the mandate to keep on "until Jesus returns." This is effected through the outreaches of more than 30 Derek Prince Offices around the world, including primary work in Australia, Canada, China, France, Germany, the Netherlands, New Zealand, Norway, Russia, South Africa, Switzerland, the United Kingdom and the United States. For current information about these and other worldwide locations, visit www.derekprince.com

Books by Derek Prince

Philosophy, the Bible and
the Supernatural
Power in the Name
Power of the Sacrifice, The
Prayers and Proclamations
Praying for the Government
Promise of Provision, The
Prophetic Guide to the
End Times
Protection from Deception
Pulling Down Strongholds
Receiving God's Best
Rediscovering God's Church
Resurrection of the Body*
Rules of Engagement
Secrets of a Prayer Warrior
Self-Study Bible Course
(revised and expanded)
Set Apart for God
Shaping History Through
Prayer and Fasting

Spiritual Warfare
Surviving the Last Days
Thanksgiving, Praise
and Worship
They Shall Expel Demons
Three Most Powerful
Words, The
Through Repentance to Faith*
Through the Psalms with
Derek Prince
Transmitting God's Power*
Three Messages for Israel
Two Harvests, The
War in Heaven
Where Wisdom Begins
Who is the Holy Spirit?
Will You Intercede?
You Matter to God
You Shall Receive Power

Get the Complete Laying the Foundations Series*

1. Founded on the Rock (B100)
2. Authority and Power of God's Word (B101)
3. Through Repentance to Faith (B102)
4. Faith and Works (B103)
5. The Doctrine of Baptisms (B104)
6. Immersion in The Spirit (B105)
7. Transmitting God's Power (B106)
8. At the End of Time (B107)
9. Resurrection of the Body (B108)
10. Final Judgment (B109)

Derek Prince Ministries
www.derekprince.com

Derek Prince Ministries Offices Worldwide

DPM – Asia/Pacific
38 Hawdon Street, Sydenham
Christchurch 8023,
New Zealand
T: + 64 3 366 4443
E: admin@dpm.co.nz
W: www.dpm.co.nz and
www.derekprince.in

DPM – Australia
Unit 21/317-321
Woodpark Road, Smithfield
New South Wales 2165,
Australia
T: + 612 9604 0670
E: enquiries@derekprince.com.au
W: www.derekprince.com.au

DPM – Canada
P. O. Box 8354 Halifax,
Nova Scotia B3K 5M1,
Canada
T: + 1 902 443 9577
E: enquiries.dpm@eastlink.ca
W: www.derekprince.org

DPM – France
B.P. 31, Route d'Oupia,
34210 Olonzac,
France
T: + 33 468 913872
E: info@derekprince.fr
W: www.derekprince.fr

DPM – Germany
Söldenhofstr. 10,
83308 Trostberg,
Germany
T: + 49-8621-64146
E: IBL.de@t-online.de
W: www.ibl-dpm.net

DPM – Netherlands
Nobelstraat 7-08
7131 PZ
Lichtenvoorde
Phone: (+31) 251-255044
E: info@dpmnederland.nl
W: www.derekprince.nl

DPM – Norway
P. O. Box 129
Lodderfjord
N-5881, Bergen,
Norway
T: +47 928 39855
E: sverre@derekprince.no
W: www.derekprince.no

Derek Prince Publications Pte. Ltd.
P. O. Box 2046,
Robinson Road Post Office,
Singapore 904046
T: + 65 6392 1812
E: dpmchina@singnet.com.sg
English web: www.dpmchina.org
Chinese web: www.ygmweb.org

DPM – South Africa
P. O. Box 33367
Glenstantia 0010 Pretoria,
South Africa
T: +27 12 348 9537
E: enquiries@derekprince.co.za
W: www.derekprince.co.za

DPM – Switzerland
Alpenblick 8
CH-8934 Knonau,
Switzerland
T: + 41(0) 44 768 25 06
E: dpm-ch@ibl-dpm.net
W: www.ibl-dpm.net

DPM – UK
PO Box 393,
Hitchin, SG5 9EU
UK
T: + 44 (0) 1462 492100
E: enquiries@dpmuk.org
W: www.dpmuk.org

DPM – USA
P. O. Box 19501
Charlotte NC 28219,
USA
T: + 1 704 357 3556
E: ContactUs@derekprince.org
W: www.derekprince.org

Other books by Derek Prince

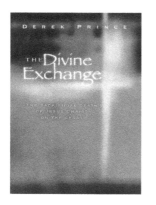

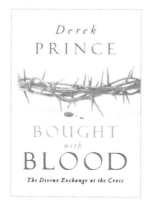

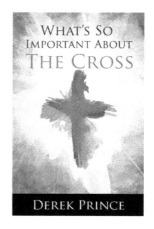

Lightning Source UK Ltd.
Milton Keynes UK
UKHW020704190520
363466UK00009B/252

9 781782 634225